A Robbie Reader

Extreme Skateboarding
with Paul Rodriguez Jr.

Marylou Morano Kjelle

Authorized
Biography

Mitchell Lane
PUBLISHERS

P.O. Box 196
Hockessin, Delaware 19707
Visit us on the web: www.mitchelllane.com
Comments? email us: mitchelllane@mitchelllane.com

Mitchell Lane PUBLISHERS

Printing   1   2   3   4   5   6   7   8   9

Extreme Sports
Extreme Cycling with Dale Homes
Extreme Skateboarding with Paul Rodriguez
Ride the Giant Waves with Garrett McNamara
Ultra Running with Scott Jurek

Library of Congress Cataloging-in-Publication Data
Kjelle, Marylou, Morano.
    Extreme skateboarding with Paul Rodriguez / by Marylou Morano Kjelle.
        p. cm. — (A Robbie reader. Extreme sports)
    Includes bibliographical references and index.
    ISBN 1-58415-489-6 (library bound)
    1. Rodriguez, Paul, 1984 — 2. Skateboarders — Biography — Juvenile literature. I. Title.
    GV859.813.R63K54 2006
    796.22 — dc22
                                                              2006022068
ISBN-10: 1-58415-489-6   ISBN-13: 9781584154891

The author would like to thank Paul Rodriguez Jr., Circe Wallace (Octagon-Athlete Manager), and Katie Sullivan (Octagon-Athlete Manager) for their help in the writing of this book.

ABOUT THE AUTHOR: Marylou Morano Kjelle is a freelance writer who lives and works in central New Jersey. She has written twenty nonfiction books for young readers and coauthored and edited others. Marylou has a master's of science degree from Rutgers University and teaches both science and writing at a community college in New Jersey.

PHOTO CREDITS: Cover, pp. 1, 3, 4 — Matt Mecaro; p. 6 — Mike Ehrman/WireImage; pp. 8, 9 — Matt Mecaro; p. 10 — Gregg DeGuire/WireImage; p. 13 — Matt Mecaro; p. 14 — Dario Rezk; pp. 16, 17 — Matt Mecaro; p. 18 — Gregg DeGuire/WireImage; p. 20 — Matt Mecaro; p. 22 — Atiba Jefferson; p. 25, 26, 27 — Matt Mecaro

PUBLISHER'S NOTE: This book has been authorized and approved for print by Paul Rodriguez Jr. It is based on personal interviews with Paul Rodriguez Jr. conducted by author Marylou Morano Kjelle in March and April 2006. While every possible effort has been made to ensure accuracy, the publisher will not assume liability for damages caused by any inaccuracies in the data.

DISCLAIMER: The sport of extreme skateboarding should not be attempted without extensive training, experience, proper protective gear, and professional assistance. This is both a high risk and dangerous sport and may result in or cause serious injury to oneself or another and may even cause death. Always consult with a trained professional in extreme skateboarding before trying this sport. Neither Mitchell Lane Publishers nor the author shall be held liable for any injuries to or damages caused by individuals attempting this sport. *Always Put Safety First.*

PLB

J-NF

TABLE OF CONTENTS

*Words in **bold type** can be found in the glossary.

Paul does a backside flip in January 2006 in Vista, California. The maneuver is a "backside" because Paul's back is to the wall (at right) as he moves from a high point to a low point.

THE BEST SKATEBOARD SUPERSTAR

The very first time Paul Rodriguez Jr. (rod-REE-gez JOO nyur) stepped on a skateboard, he knew his life would never be the same. Nothing compared to the **sensation** (sen-SAY-shun) of flying that he felt as he soared off a ledge with his skateboard tucked between his feet.

Paul had one goal in life. He wanted to be a street skateboard superstar.

But he didn't want to be just any skateboard superstar. He wanted to be like his idols, Eric Koston and Tom Penny. Both had won many

Paul's ability to soar over hedges helped him win a gold medal at X Games XI at the Staples Center in Los Angeles in August 2005.

awards and medals for skateboarding. To Paul, they were the best. Paul wanted to be the best, too.

Each year in August, special sports competitions called the X Games are held in Los Angeles, California. The *X* stands for *extreme,* because the sports played involve risky stunts. Vert skateboarding is one extreme sport. It involves skateboarding off single ramps and U-shaped ramps called half pipes. Street skateboarding is also an extreme sport. Street skateboarders do tricks on benches, ledges, and hand rails. They perform fancy **maneuvers** (muh-NOO-vurs) like the kickflip. A kickflip is spinning the skateboard while it is in the air. Another maneuver is the ollie, where the skateboarder stomps the back of the skateboard and slides his or her foot to the nose while the board soars through the air.

All eyes were on Paul at the X Games on August 4, 2005. It was his turn to compete in the Men's Street Skateboarding Competition. The year before, Paul had won a gold medal at this competition. Now his fans were eager to see if he could do it again.

The crowd roared as Paul began the last of his routines. For fifteen minutes he kept the crowd at the edge of their seats with his skateboard maneuvers. He did kickflips, he rode his skateboard down stairs, and he launched himself from ledges. He sailed down railings on two skateboard wheels.

Twisting and turning this way and that, Paul and his skateboard flew over **obstacles** as though he had wings. He was competing against other skateboard champions, but no one could match his skill. When the scores were totaled at the end of the game, Paul's score was the highest. Once again Paul had won the X Games Men's Street Skateboarding Competition. For the second year in a row, Paul Rodriguez Jr. was the best skateboard superstar.

For a frontside kickflip, Paul faces the stairs while kicking his skateboard into a spin. He then lands back on it.

Paul Junior has learned a lot about following his dream from his father, Paul Rodriguez Sr. Father and son got together for a movie opening in May 2005.

A FAMOUS FATHER

Paul Rodriguez Jr. was born on December 31, 1984, in Tarzana, California. His father is the **comedian** (kuh-MEE-dee-in) Paul Rodriquez Sr., and his mother is Laura Martinez.

Paul Rodriguez Sr. was born in Mexico. He came to the United States with his family when he was three years old. He and his six brothers and sisters moved from place to place, picking crops with their parents. The work was hard and the hours were long.

Paul Senior wanted to give his family a better life. He left farmwork to enter show business. Later, he became one of the first

Latino television and movie stars in the United States. He also became a **television producer.**

Paul Junior has a sister, Nikole, who is five years older, and a half brother, Lucas, who is fifteen years younger. When Paul was six years old, his father started building his show business career. He traveled from state to state, and Paul did not see him often. From that point on, Paul lived mostly with his mother in California's San Fernando Valley. She is an actress and a script supervisor.

Whenever Paul and his father were able to spend the day together, Paul Senior's fans were usually around, asking for his **autograph.** Young Paul never seemed to have his father to himself.

Today, Paul and his father are the best of friends. But back then, it was very difficult to have a famous father.

Paul was eleven years old when he noticed the kids in his neighborhood skateboarding. "It looked like they were having a great time," said Paul. That year he purchased a Powell skateboard

It takes a lot of energy to be the best street skateboard superstar. Paul enjoys a break from skateboarding in Los Angeles in June 2006.

with his Christmas money. Once he had a skateboard, he used it whenever he could.

Paul also skateboarded *wherever* he could, including inside the house. One day he tried skateboarding off the coffee table and broke it. "Why were you skating in the house?" Paul Senior asked. "Because it is raining out," said young Paul.

13

A picnic table is not only for eating! In the world of extreme street skateboarding, everyday objects are used for performing tricks.

"P-ROD"

The older Paul got, the more important skateboarding became to him. As a teenager, he did not care about eating or sleeping. He let his schoolwork slide. When he tried to study, he couldn't remember what he had just read. All he could think about was being on his skateboard. That was all he wanted to do.

Paul grew to be 5 feet 8 inches tall and 110 pounds. Having such a light frame helped him keep his balance on the skateboard. It also helped him keep his tricks fast and clean. Soon his friends were calling him P-Rod.

Loading docks are great places to practice street skateboarding. Paul practices his frontside kickflip at a loading dock in Oxnard, California.

Paul skateboarded with a team called the City Stars. The team would practice on the loading dock of a grocery store in Los Angeles. The loading dock became Paul's training ground. He practiced every skateboard trick he could think of there.

By the time he was fifteen years old, Paul knew he wanted to make skateboarding his career, but no one took him seriously. Paul's father wanted him to become an actor like him. "Skateboarding? Where is that going to get you?" he asked his son.

Paul didn't listen to his father. He had already made up his mind to devote his life to skateboarding. He quit Birmingham High School when he was in the tenth grade. There would be nothing standing in the way of Paul and his skateboard.

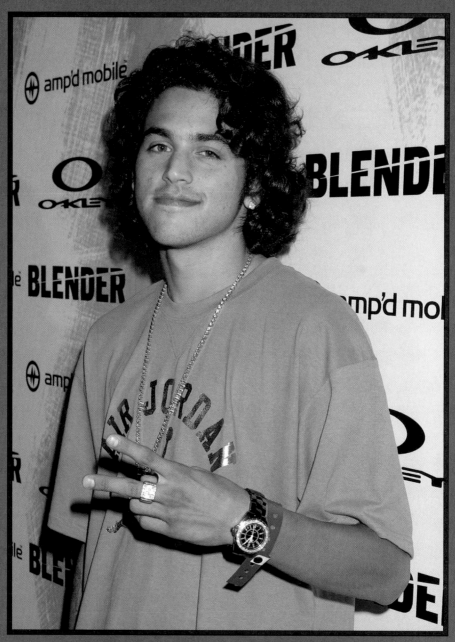

Paul participated in the X Games for the fourth time in 2006. He gave the peace sign at an X Games kickoff party before the games got under way on August 3.

TURNING PRO

Slowly Paul Senior began to realize how much skateboarding skill and talent his son had. He also remembered when he was a young man. He had wanted to make his mark on the world by entering show business, and his own father had not approved.

Eventually, Paul Senior came around to seeing things Paul Junior's way. He let his son devote all his time to the thing he loved the best. "I'm proud of him," Paul Senior now says.

In 2002, when Paul was seventeen years old, he turned **professional.** His manager helped him get sponsored by two teams, the City Stars and ES.

Slam City Jam is a series of skateboard championship games held in British Columbia,

The front part of a skateboard is called its nose, and skating down the edge of an obstacle is called grinding. Paul does a switch stance frontside nosegrind in Los Angeles.

Canada. This event was the first in which Paul competed as a professional skateboarder. He came in third place in the Men's Street Skating competition. His prize was $5,000.

In 2003, Paul was named Rookie of the Year by *Transworld SKATEboarding Magazine.* That same year, he entered the X Games for the first time. He won third place—a bronze medal—in the Street Skating Competition. In 2004, Paul won his first gold medal at the X Games. He beat one of his idols, Eric Koston, who had won a medal in each of the previous five years.

One interviewer asked Paul when he really felt like he had "made it" as a pro skater. He responded, "When I got in a video game." The first video game in which Paul was featured was *Tony Hawk Underground.* Tony Hawk is a vert skateboard legend. He has won six X Games gold medals.

Paul liked playing himself in the video game. He said it felt like he had his own character already made up.

Paul performs a hardflip by rotating his skateboard while flying through the air.

TAKING IT TO
THE EXTREME

Paul Rodriguez Jr. is one of the highest paid skateboarders in the world. In addition to the money he earns in competitions, he also **endorses** products like Plan B Skateboards and Mountain Dew soda. He also has his own Nike **signature** shoe. Paul is the first skateboarder to have his own Nike shoe. Nike spokesman Kevin Imamura calls Paul "an absolutely amazing athlete."

Paul's career as a skateboarder allows him to have a beautiful home in the Chatsworth section of Los Angeles, California. He can travel the world and buy almost anything he wants.

Paul's fans are extremely important to him. Paul always tries to take the time to speak to them and to give them his autograph. Treating his fans with respect is something he learned from his father. "Sometimes I see myself and [I think] whoa, this is how my dad acts," he said.

Paul is also talented at thinking up new skateboarding tricks. He doesn't always give his tricks a name, but when he combines flips, twists, and spins on his skateboard, his moves are uniquely (yoo-NEEK-lee) his. "There's no limits, there's no rules. . . . Whatever your brain can think of, you can do it, man," he says.

Although Paul did not return to high school, he tries to educate himself. He enjoys reading **biographies** and watching the History Channel. Maybe someday he will continue his

When a skateboard's front wheels and nose are locked in a position on top of an obstacle, the trick is called a noseblunt slide. Picnic tables are good obstacles for performing this trick.

A heelflip lets the skateboarder stop the board with his feet while pulling up his knees. Paul performed this trick on a set of steps in Los Angeles in April 2006.

education. "I always want to be . . . bettering myself," Paul says in a quiet way.

Another possible career that Paul sees for himself is acting. Now that he has made it on his own as a skateboarder, he is more open to accepting help from his father, and acting is something that interests him.

Whether he keeps on as a street skateboard superstar or becomes an actor, Paul will continue to work hard to reach his goals. He wants to show all young people, especially young Latinos, that everyone can be a winner. And no matter what he does in life, Paul Rodriguez Jr. will take it to the extreme!

CHRONOLOGY

1984	Paul Rodriguez Jr. is born on December 31.
1990	Paul's father, Paul Rodriguez Sr., begins traveling; Paul does not see very much of him.
1995	Paul buys his first skateboard with money he received for Christmas.
1999	Paul quits high school to become a full-time skateboarder.
2002	Paul participates in his first professional event, Slam City Jam; he wins third place.
2003	Paul enters the X Games for the first time and wins a bronze medal in street skateboarding.
2004	Paul wins his first gold medal at the X Games.
2005	Paul wins his second gold medal at the X Games.
2006	Paul takes seventh place at the X Games.

SELECTED MOVIES AND VIDEO GAMES

2006	*A Time to Shine* (DVD)
	Thursday Theater (DVD)
2005	*American Wasteland* (aka *Tony Hawk's American Wasteland*) (video game)
	Firsthand (DVD)
	The Forecast (DVD)
	Subtleties (DVD)
2004	*FKD Bearings* (DVD)
	On Tap (DVD)
2003	*In Bloom* (DVD)
	Underground (aka *Tony Hawk's Pro Skater 5*) (video game)
	Yeah Right! (DVD)

GLOSSARY

autograph	(AW-tuh-graf)—to sign your name to something; also, a name signed to something.
biographies	(by-AH-grah-feez)—stories about people's lives.
comedian	(kuh-MEE-dee-in)—an entertainer who tells jokes.
endorses	(en-DOR-ses)—talks about or uses a product in order to increase sales.
maneuvers	(muh-NOO-vurs)—moves one makes when performing tricks.
obstacles	(OB-stih-kuls)—things that are in the way.
professional	(pruh-FEH-shuh-nul)—someone who is paid for what he or she does.
sensation	(sen-SAY-shun)—a feeling.
signature	(SIG-nah-chur)—(of a product) a brand that advertises someone's name.
television producer	(TEH-leh-vih-jun proh-DOO-sir)—someone whose job is to get a television show on the air.

FIND OUT MORE

Books

Brooke, Michael. *The Concrete Wave: The History of Skateboarding.* Toronto: Warwick House Publishing, 1999.

Crossingham, John. *Extreme Skateboarding.* New York: Crabtree Publishing Company, 2003.

Kjelle, Marylou Morano. *Tony Hawk: Pro Skateboarder.* Hockessin, Delaware: Mitchell Lane Publishers, 2004.

Savage, Jeff. *The X Games: Skateboarding's Greatest Event.* Mankato, Minnesota: Edge Books, 2004.

Werner, Doug. *Skateboarder's Start-Up: A Beginner's Guide to Skateboarding.* San Diego, California: Tracks Publishing, 2000.

Works Consulted

This book is based on the author's personal interviews with Paul Rodriguez Jr. in March and April of 2006.

Aguila, Justino. "Comic Looks Back on a Life of Fame, Disappointment and Growth." *The Orange County Register,* June 22, 2004.

Bonsignore, Vincent. "Getting the Last Laugh: Chatsworth Resident Rodriguez a Success in Skateboarding." *The Daily News of Los Angeles,* August 6, 2005, p. S1.

Cave, Steve. "P Rod Comes of Age at X Games X." http://skateboard.about.com/od/evets/a/XGamesXPRod.htm

Gonzales, John. "Junior Shows He's No Joke." *Press Enterprise,* August 6, 2004, p. C01.

Higgins, Matt. "Actor's Son Is on His Own 2 Feet, Sometimes." *The New York Times,* August 5, 2005, p. D6.

Pearson, Ryan. "King of Street Skateboarding Son of Comedian Rodriguez." *Deseret News,* August 7, 2005, p. A02. http://deseretnews.com/dn/view/ 0,1249,600154140,00.html

Ramirez, Steve. "X Games Notebook: Rodriguez Makes Dad Proud. " *The Daily News of Los Angeles,* August 6, 2004, p. S3.

Real Sports with Bryant Gumbel. Interview with Paul Rodriguez; transcript, November 1, 2005.

"Rodriguez Does a Double-Take." ESPN Press Release http://skateboard.about.co/od/evets/a/ XGames11MSF.htm

Ruibal, Sal. "Comedian's Son Is Having the Last Laugh." *USA Today,* March 29, 2005, p. 3C.

Swanson, Mirjam. "X Games Notebook: Rodriguez Smokes Competition." *Press Enterprise,* August 5, 2005, p. C03.

On the Internet

Paul Rodriguez
   http://www.paulrodriguez.com/pauljr.htm

Streetboardz.com
   http://www.streetboardz.com/parojrprosk.html

"X Games" Player biography: Paul Rodriguez
   http://expn.go.com/expn/summerx/2004/ athleteBio?id=5575

INDEX